# IDENTITY THEORY
## NEW AND SELECTED POEMS, 1980-2010

# IDENTITY THEORY
## NEW AND SELECTED POEMS, 1980-2010

BY

DOROTHY WALL

BLUE LIGHT PRESS • 1ST WORLD LIBRARY

1st WORLD
PUBLISHING

SAN FRANCISCO • FAIRFIELD • DELHI

IDENTITY THEORY
NEW AND SELECTED POEMS, 1980-2010
Copyright ©2011 by Dorothy Wall

For information contact:

1ST WORLD PUBLISHING
809 S. 2nd Street
Fairfield, IA 52556
www.1stworldpublishing.com

BLUE LIGHT PRESS
1563 45th Avenue
San Francisco, CA 94122

COVER, ILLUSTRATIONS, BOOK DESIGN:
Melanie Gendron
www.MelanieGendron.com

AUTHOR PHOTO:
Jane Scherr

AUTHOR WEBSITE:
www.dorothywall.com

FIRST EDITION

LCCN: 2011963153

ISBN 9781421886428

# Also by Dorothy Wall

*Encounters with the Invisible: Unseen Illness,*
*Controversy, and Chronic Fatigue Syndrome* (2005)

*Hanging the Mapmaker* (2003, poems)

*Finding Your Writer's Voice:*
*A Guide to Creative Fiction* (1994, coauthor)

*Unfinished* (1993, poems)

# Acknowledgments

I'm indebted to many mentors and friends who have helped me grapple with this thing called poetry, and have fun, too. At San Francisco State in the late 70s, I studied with Stan Rice, Mark Linenthal, Kathleen Fraser. Members of the Berkeley Poets Coop Workshop in the late 70s and 80s were a shaping influence, especially Charles Entrekin, Bruce Hawkins, Stewart Florsheim, as were members of several poetry groups in the 80s and early 90s, including among others, Ramsay Bell Breslin, Elise Morgan, Thaisa Frank, Pat Dientsfry. As always, my grateful appreciation to husband Bill Barnes and daughter Lisa Swatt for their insightful feedback, love and support over all these years. My thanks to the following journals in which a number of these poems first appeared, some in earlier versions.

"Sweeping," "Our Kind of Fun: Midlife," "Joy," "Things I'd Never Tell My Mother," "Marin Hillside, 1975," *PoetryMagazine.com*, Winter 2011

"Cleaning in Spanish," *The Dos Passos Review*, Vol. 7, No. 2, Spring 2011

"Left," *Natural Bridge*, No. 10, Fall 2003

"Magnified," "Starting Out, Carrying On," *JAMA:The Journal of the American Medical Association*, Nov. 20, 2002

"The Unhealed," *Cimarron Review*, Issue 140, Summer 2002

"Hanging the Mapmaker," "Sleeping with Books," *River Oak Review*, No. 15, 16, Winter 2000, Spring 2001

"Visits," *Coracle*, No. 8, 9, Millennium Issue, 2000

"The Gaze We Bring with Us," *Bottomfish Magazine*, Vol. 14, Winter 1993

"The Quilters," *Hudson Valley Echoes*, No. 27, Winter 1992-93

"Map of Earthquakes," *Blue Unicorn*, Vol. XII, No. 2, February 1989

"The Daily Life of Nuns," *Prairie Schooner*, Vol. 61, No. 2, Summer 1987

"Draft," *Berkeley Poets Cooperative #14*, 1978. Reprinted in *California Living, The Magazine of the San Francisco Sunday Examiner & Chronicle*, April 15, 1979, and in *Berkeley Poets Cooperative Anthology 1970-1980*, 1980.

"Beginning" was published in the anthology *Wedding Blessings: Prayers and Poems Celebrating Love, Marriage and Anniversaries*, ed. by June Cotner (Broadway Books/Random House, 2003).

# IDENTITY THEORY
## NEW AND SELECTED POEMS, 1980-2010

# Contents

## 3. Zane and Zoe Poems—2003-2010

## 4. New Poems—2003-2010

For Bill and Lisa, who sustain me

For Zane and Zoe, who give me hope

# 1.

## From *Unfinished*—1980s

# Sweeping

We live under the litter of the eucalyptus.
I can't sweep it out of my mother's
bed or the pockets of my children.

Leaves like scythes, tin-green and fragrant,
dirt funnels always surprising me.
The side yard, the front yard, upper yard,
the rooms inside.  People arrive at my door
while I sweep, people I know from
earlier times, men and women and children
in their suits and dresses with their
faces that say, 'here we are,' men who
forgive me when I kiss them, though
I've done nothing to forgive, my own
children who stare at me, wondering
if they're mine, smiling and shifting
feet.  I hold my broom, uncertain
who to greet.

# The Gaze We Bring with Us

Father carries his suitcase
out the door, mother's forehead
pressed to the door edge.

Then this: the chain-link fence,
fingers clutching cold
wires, the open stairs I was afraid
of falling through, house
on a cliff, car pulling
up to the edge, mother's skirt
lifted in the updraft before she

bundled us home.  I didn't live
in a place where the land fell
away, I came for a visit
and left, taking the empty
air for my solitude.

Holding so much I forgot
lightness, hoped for an
offering plate passed by hands
so my pockets, stretched
at the seams, could become
less weighted.  Lifting
my gaze, I wanted to climb
the highest steeple,
wondered what door led
to the top, the dark, a hand
over my eyes.

# The Quilters

These are the strides we take
while children sleep.
Now we spread the white cloth.
We break open a rose petal by petal.
One hundred stitches shape
the edge of a leaf.  From our
hands, a lattice of stars, hollyberries,
baskets, vines, drawn into the heavens
where they'll stay despite all
that goes on under and above them.

Patience, obedience, stillness.
The skies compose on our laps
spun from a willingness to sit
to know the pores of cloth
the weave of breath that slips
from children's mouths, the breath
of galaxies, their trails of dust
pulling together, our heads
surrounding the world.

# Blackout, 1944

It was a job he could do, left
home with the women.  On what
street?  I can't picture
my father's gas-masked face peering
into doorways to remind
Pull your blackout shades.

        I was not born
when he worked with such vigilance
to sheet his town, pushing night
into a darkness before cities,
before sound, as I was turning
in some unknown sky.  I can't see
his expression, or the odd lilt
to his head-heavy walk, I can only

imagine him stalking each
brown-yellow glow, not even
the thin beam of a flashlight
allowed, until every crack
was shuttered.

Some lessons are not learned,
they're simply found
in the deep illumination of sleep.
When arms gathered me, dressed me,
already I knew the necessity
of seeing.  I turned my head
to a square of light.
Here, I start remembering.

# The Daily Life of Nuns

I stand in an ocean, my feet planted
at the bottom where algae spread
their blues and greens, my body
stretched into the spinning air.
I am still as a curved shell.

          When the vesper
bells ring and the ocean is a field
of grain with low flung light and white
draped heads moving in files,
I feel lonely.

          I must remember
my pewter cup, the level of the
water, the shadow along the edge
when I tilt it, the dark
angle where it becomes a coolness
on the inside but nothing
I can see.  It is simple then.
I love the path the cup leaves
in the air and sing into it
with the others, hold
the bread wrapped in cloth
and feel silent as
disappearing water.

## Map of Earthquakes

Inside a glass case the earth
fans its layers like underskirts,
a red flag at each spot where the sediment
wouldn't stay down, where trees funneled
into their roots, where cats

tumbled, feet up, where houses,
sticks thrown on the ground,
became strange signs of a new order.

# The Peacefulness of Statuary

## 1

Risen from a slow chipping away,
each creamy curl reducing
skin to the skin below.  She is all
skin, unveined,
she has no need of blood.
We believe in her like the
unbroken surface of milk.

## 2

Eyes, mouth sealed,
she lifts her arm,
holds aside marble folds
exposing the white undersheen,
a monument to the art of
disrobing and remaining
sheathed.

From arched streams of water in
greenish light she
steps, one foot
settled in air as if
anything could find its place by
holding still long enough.
In full view, the splendid
idea of her, a gaze
she steps out of
smooth as stone.

3

Violence slow as
chisel's even stroke—
So much is expected of her,
a thin steel spike in the
sole of one foot holding her
in place.

She lives in water and air,
heats and cools to the rhythm
of sun, moon, bodies that do not
ask her to stir.

What falls over her is light and dark
and a curious hand that strokes
her unmoving foot.

4

Where a beam of water flattens
against an iron scepter,
the slow green bleed of
ore down her ivory leg.

Even as hands scraped each limb bone clean
a thin stain washed down.
Now she can only be pure in moonlight.

5

For all the reverence given
her breast will not soften.
You cannot pull her in, cannot
suck her mouth open, your tongue
hooking hers.  If she
stepped into your arms, supple
at last, you would hold
slivers of stone.

# Draft

We stuffed paper in all the cracks
then old rags,
the wool rug.

Where have we come to
that precautions do not hold,
that even in light
your face is a confusion to me.

I cannot sense the direction of this wind
that flaps and drives against our house
like the things we deny inside ourselves.

# The Return

Wet leaves scratching the windowpane,
pouring the milk, mother's face caught
in lamplight, the child in bed awaiting
the glass

the white glass moving through the hallway,
rain pouring down rooftops,
down oil-slicked streets

the child reaching, mother in the doorway
hesitates, head bent as if
listening to a story
she has heard a hundred times

a puzzling story, painful, joyous,
a story she loves the way we
love our own lives simply
because they're ours.

## At My Side

Two thousand voices singing
"If I had a hammer" and
my daughter sleeps.

In balcony's close breath
and heat, more comforting than

arms, her head slips back
mouth open
as if waiting to be fed.

It's song that pours into
her living sleep,
phrase, beat   she takes in
her own way
open as a hole in the sky.

Each time I bring her somewhere
she takes me further.

At my side, proof of grace
the place
I would rest.

> Pete Seeger concert
> Berkeley Community Theater
> February 1984

# Unfinished

Our feet leave chalky tracks
across the concrete floor,
airport wing under construction.

We're early. We'll wait
in a disarray of nails,
ladders, carpet in fat rolls,
strange witnesses to my daughter's
leaving. These objects will remain
with me. She is already

gone, her perfect profile
stunningly her own, poised,
only a slight ripple
of energy beneath skin
like taut muscle before the gate
breaks open.

On its tiny strip the plane waits,
the grey-carpeted passageway
empty for her.

The loud speaker cracks.
An engine shudders the windows.
She leans forward as if
diving, pure pleasure ahead.
Red twirl of skirt, tossed smile,
like something thrown away
I wasn't through with.

What is to me speed and distance
to her is as still as the view
from inside an egg, where
everything slowly unfolds
as it should. Such order.

14

# 2.

From *Hanging the Mapmaker*—
1990s and early 2000s

# Left

I was reading when I heard the fisted slam
leapt to see the pigeon's reeling, back-pedaled flight
its intimate body oiled on glass

as if instead of giving itself
with instant blind might it had
posed for days while an artist's

fine-tipped brush lined each breast-feather
one by one in banks of overlapping
fringe, a hint of beak pressed to chest

suggestive and spare, that eye, white and
bare, a bony upswept wing.
Each morning sun illuminates the ghostly

moment its swooping, unplanned
path quickly changed.  I'm left
to witness, aren't we all, what I choose—

the whacked, unsettled stare
bristled plume, brush-stroke wing, all there
until early rains.

## Sleeping with Books

We buy books we will never read
and keep them by our bed.
We sleep better this way

in a room piled with words, ellipses
passions, electricities, stacked
on bedside tables, dusty shelves

amassed on the cedar chest where the
cat nests, all those
epiphanies, their specter

and possibility around our heads.
Theories of civility, virility,
Faust's wager met

Darcy's wedding set,
that intoxicating moment pen leapt
those mercurial flights

we collect.
They would be aghast
those thousands of minds

at their questionable, cobwebby fate
as ballast to our dreams
but we appreciate

lucidity subsided into consecutive
lines, into grammar, Times Roman
this strange and soothing weight

as our minds slip into that
other intelligence, uncontained
inchoate.

# Dreaming in Florence

What sculptors chisel from stone
surely I can carve from sleep.
I'm deep in the hand-hewn mines

where stone crumbles before a shape
appears.  I'm dreaming
of taking my daughter to the city

of cathedrals, rolling uneven tiles
catching the faces of saints
in hues they never wore.

I'm taking her face where I can
see it in the light tossed
from a thousand white tiles

where above the Medici tombs
women with q-tips clear the eyes of
Day and Night so we can see anew

their wild rememberings,
where I'm once more young,
her shiny eyes locked on my

moving hands, where I can
hear again the steady hew
of her growing.

# Magnified

I can't look at blown-up photos of granular cells
gritty microbial budding and bulging, furry
tufts, pustulant fissures give me the shivers

fascinated though I am by minuscule life
the unseen rife with our hope
or our nemesis, depending,
perhaps even our ending,

all the things we have in us, greater
than the Guinness Book of Records and more
startling.  We carry our share of the planet
as we're meant to, but falsely chaste
purveyors of good taste we fail

to mention the riotous convention
within, a perilous forgetting of what lies
where we avert our eyes, that
bulbous teeming fecund overblown busyness
unconcerned with charity, vying
for posterity.

# Young Lives

When we were young my daughter and I
lived for awhile in a moldy dive

where mice scuttled loud as elephants
in the walls, their exuberance

made us shiver, and that nightly chomping
unnerving accompaniment to tromping

seemed proof of our inglorious days
surrounded by tiny teeth, invisible meals

we didn't want to imagine.  Now grown
my daughter has imaginings of her own

wondering if the scrabbling behind her plaster
could be another tiny-toed disaster

the trunk of her car is damp, floorboards, too
mold powdering the carpet blue

*Remember our Vega?* water sloshing in the trunk
grass grew there, truly, we lived with funk

I was too exhausted to care.
She's spending a little time there

in that place called scraping by
I can hear the catch in her voice, the high

scratching pause.  She's thinking
of dry floors, solid walls, imagining

adulthood, please God
without the maws and paws.

# Our Kind of Fun: Midlife

Evenings, when the halfway day
closes and opens, when we step
into streets as sun submerges,
streetlights bloom and the fracas
of the world holds its
half-promise of loss and
possibility, when

it can go any way, we leave
unfinished a dim sky and settle
while we can in the flick of
bedroom light, metamorphic and
complete.  Garnet clarity of wine,
slung arm, pillow and news.
I'd rather.  He prefers.
Nothing we can't agree on
familiar as we are with this
coupled state, a luxurious
toe-stretching yawn
expounding upon the orange
disappearing day, aware of
brokenness and failings and
these moments of being spared.

# Betty at the Door

She's got one leg and a terrible question.
Easier to help an animal in need,
but this.  Up the ladder I hang from

on the rung of *you never know* and
*drugs* and *it's not my* she looks tiny
in her creaky wheelchair and I feel too large
too high up here where I'm getting tired.

I want to climb down, hand her the question
to settle accounts, but that would make me
small and besides, I can't figure

right and wrong in their disguise.
Who owes?  Who gives?  It's a hard tussle
between our hearts, I'm no good at this.
Nothing I can say will equal the eloquence

of her warning, that white-socked stump
carried like a sidewalk-skimming cane
alert to what's ahead.

It touches ordinary things, recognizes
them instantly through a tremor
up the spine.  She needs four dollars,
needs it bad.

# Hanging the Mapmaker

In 1603, having lost a galleon along
the coast of Upper California, and
having found no safe harbor, the Viceroy
of New Spain, in the name of the King,
ordered the mapmaker hanged.

He only did what a mapmaker does,
give shape to a king's desire.
A careful artist, faithful
to the heart, he'd wake

early, take up his pen
so the King, asleep,
could continue to dream.

Crooked back of land, ruinous sea,
discarded for a green
expansive shore.  Pity

the mapmaker, touching
his finger to the
windy coast of our

longing, letting us believe
we can match dream
to land, or that with map
in hand we'll see

the contours true.
He couldn't sketch this world
with only an earthly view.
Trained to sight what was imagined

he never saw bounty not yet
visited by dream,
beyond a fog-hung bay
the seamed, gold-laden hills.

He sailed on.
Desire always does.

# Virus

A packet of survival, instructions for how
to keep going with no angst, no afterthought
pure voracious forwardness inscribed on whatever
cannot repel it, the perfect mechanism
for sacking cities.

# The Unhealed

"Wanting to look again.
Into the patient face of the unhealed."
—Eavan Boland

As if injury could rest.
As if those mending—who isn't—

aren't rattling with repair.
Homeostatic imperative.

Cellular scrambling. Wounds
are hothouses of activity

lavishly nursed, swelling
with anger, love, want

defying sleep.
The body that appears

settled in its losses—
old sweatshirt, honeyed tea

an evening's news and rice—
incubates a molecular heat

shrill as the kettle
the visceral drive not to abide

injury's disrepair.
Beneath a placid stretch

the insurrection of the flesh
as in a steamy room

injury wrestles on, devoted
to its own alarm.

27

# Starting Out, Carrying On

The freshness, the expanse,
clean linen floating to the
waiting bed.

Who else does possibility belong to
if not the ill, returned

to that place of birthing, white-gowned,
awash with fever and philosophy
and a tendency to conversion.

Bathed in sweat such cleansing
seems possible, even divined,
the white rind of moon

casting a line I'll cross
come morning, this time better,
this time different.

To be consumed by fever
what does that mean?
I wake, dreaming of water

hot bones of my back leave
their damp-sheeted impression.

I'm still here
in this hollow by repetition formed
waiting for release
from the slow victory
of history.

# Beginning

After I do, toasts, tears
songs and kisses, after this

comes love's long reward,
an unrolling of hours you'll

regard one day, surprised
at the world they've made.

Today your view is ahead,
the unplanned forest

your own.  Today you take up
against the unknown

love's torch, its warmth
and blaze, its solace, its strange

equations: the more closely held,
the more wide flung,

the more given, the more gathered.
Long have you been approaching

this mysterious dim grove.
Now you step, arms linked,

carrying fire and comfort, into
the lit trees rich

with fruit and seeds
waiting for you.

## Visits

My mother visits more now
than when she was alive, her voice
strung along the ribs of dreams

these bones she gave me.
At first her restlessness shook
my nights.  I wandered
from home to home

doors open, windows unscreened
rooms rearranged or empty
only a chimney left
old hearth

what lasts when all else
burns.  I was drifting
to the heart of things
startled by scents—
baby sweetness of apple juice
putrid bitterness of skunk
cold air grazing my cheek.
It's not what I
expected, this touching
and reaching.

It's quieter now.
I'm settling in, accepting
what she offers—
sweetness, bitterness
the universe's breath.
She's given me the whole of it
nothing less.

# At Mother's Grave

She's on the loose again
she's been dispatched
or I have, to leave what is known
though we still land in each
other's arms, these
carrying, holding arms
a solace even in dream.

We try to place all sorrows
in a furrow, or burn them
but they burrow their way
to air, restless and risen.
She wants to accompany me, that's all
tromping about for explanation
for a life collapsed into
bible entry, tomb and grass
my boots cross-hatched
with sloughed blades.

I've released what I can.
This weight of traveling
alone or together
back to earth
It's harder than you think
she whispers.

## Mother's Voice

The slivered voice made clear
a hurtling hurt and a need

for tending.  We tended, my sisters and I,
those high-ceilinged sobs,

fury leveled into a tip-toe day
until an eerie silence settled.

We held that silence like a tray of glass
but this one defeats us, this silence

too vast to fix with love fiercely given.
My sister and I sob on the phone.

When we desire noise death unfurls its long
strange hush and all its clamoring.

In dreams my mother yells at me for
not listening, but I am.  I drop everything

to grasp the voice I've managed to save in
tangled ganglia, neural flash, my skull

cradling her flares like a struck
match in a cupped hand.  When I crave

something I miss, I always have
that scratching flared kiss.

# Compiling My Father's Biography
# for His Memorial Service

Children's births. Degrees,
Promotions.  The father who
carried me up a roadside
snowbank becomes a margin note
or was my sister perched
on his hip?  We had matching
coats and fistfuls of wet
red-fingered bliss, snow-soaked
knees, to young, all of us, to be
diminished or numbed by whiteness
we flung ourselves in it
gripped by enthusiasm for departure
a road trip, winter.
After he left came forty-two years
of letters.  Birthdays.
Christmas.  Accumulations of loss
I sort and ply with the eye
of the dispossessed.  I hold them
to the light this grey morning
of my task, thin slivers:
a volunteer job, a day of aspens
not much happening, New York,
Atlanta, where was he?  The dead
take their omissions while we
flounder through reconstruction
this unreliable, dry landscape
a eulogy to incompletion.
I prod my sisters for stories, facts.
All those disquieting days will not
appear, all those fervors
banked by a generous snow.
Here they are
simplified like any truth
we try to know.

# 3.

Zane and Zoe Poems—2003-2010

# Enough

On Third Avenue the universe has shrunk to a
face-tightening wail, he's eight days and

everything pales beside the volume of his
cataclysmic need, the scramble to undo

blouse and buttons.  What can his mind
find to dream other than appetite and

greed, empty as it is of the demands
of patience.  We who understand

forbearance, who are steeped in silence
and forgotten dreams, rush to quiet

the tongue still learning to form
its outrage, still finding in lung

and breath a handy snare
to assure the reign of desire

and flesh, the mouth-stuffing breast
trickle and warmth, snuffling

and sighing, jerky breath
for now, it's enough.

                                    June 12, 2003

# In Daddy's Hands

Up-ended, mitted feet
hair-clutching shriek

furious paddling, a diving
nose tickle,

raucous delight
in flight.

If life were this—before
gravity and floors, dusty

corridors—a lunging
hummingbird dip

into the upturned face he knows
by scent, vaulting

through the air-arc
of his little life

as untried as this impromptu lift
that slowly forming

engine of a self made of
just such hovering.

March 2004

# First Words

This January our garden's drab and damp, and the world
open to his blazing mind.  He weaves

bends to clutch a rock, staggers off, reels back
to twigs, a soggy tennis ball, plants

his velcro shoes on flagstone, *mmm*, neck tensed
fists plunged sideways, *mmm*, face straining

from the concentrated heat within.  The day glints
with future knowing, the cascade to come, a flash

of chemicals, *mmm*, a split-second spark, *mmmMA*
explodes with a rapture of accomplishment, wide-eyed

glee, a drunken stumble to mama's legs grasped
at the knee, another *mmm* building in his throat.

January 2005

# Where's He

A question only he could ask
flinging his body into jungle's lush
path behind rattan palm,
Japanese hibiscus, his voice

piping through broad-leafed
African banana in greenhouse's
snug earthiness, *Where's he?*
suspended like the quivering
droplet at leaf tip.

A dangling heater huffs
tropical air, scarlet bracts
gleam.  In this dense arboreal
nest, he knows exactly
how his universe is formed, knows
the answering voices will chime

*Where's he?  Where's Zane?*
*I don't see him*, knows the shivering,
held excitement, the gap-toothed,
squealing tumble out from hiding
*There he is!* will always be seen
no philosophy more certain

no discovery as assured,
to be found again and again
the compass of his universe always pointed
to him, the hot-breathed stalks,
mulch-soaked air letting him
out to daylight.

Mother's Day, 2005

# Joy

O slug, O little baby slug
gluey with mucous shine
delivered with a grandson's glee—
slug on grandma's arm!

Under bricks, under stones
he probes, through wild onions dense
with the promise of crawliness.
The yard's upturned and heaved
strewn by fingers lusting for
slime and wiggly.

He's onto snails, suctioned
to a daylily stem, a trove
of oozing husks gathered with
furious joy, as eggs on Easter,
those blunt antennae,
stretched necks, waving their
slow panic from the depths
of his plastic cup.  He defeats
each snaily climb with a
finger push, counts his
riches in the clack of shells
and we haven't mentioned the worms.

O worms, O snails,
better than our tired tales.
When morning newspaper brings
its sadnesses, its wars, and a

stuckfast drifter washed
up on these strange shores,
I lift the sticky rider on a
fingertip, escort it,
periscoping the air, to its
leafy escape, there to
settle in, to await
its glorious discovery.

October 2007

## Survival of the Fittest

*Allosauruses have horns*, he points
to the nubs, *Tyrannosaurus rex don't*

informing us sadly ignorant
grandparents who can't tell one

from the other, but nonetheless cheer
every plastic, hurled foe in this

Olympian battle, every smashed
snout, each T. rex charge.

We have the best backyard
in the neighborhood, where the

terrors of the world are resolved
before snack time and yellow-bellied

Allosaurus, feet up, is not
as terminal as he seems, where

the bludgeoned and bitten revive
perhaps to race motorcycles.

Stegosaurus referees, declaring it
T. rex's day, and they all prance off

to lunch, smacking cashew butter
through snorts and neighs, forgetting

the fury that drove them. They'll settle
for being small and surrounded

by a rather benign day after all,
with its sunlit graces, future races.

When that asteroid slammed into grassy plains
smothering the dinosaurs in its fist of dust

only small adaptable animals survived.
We have the proof.

April 2008

# Won't

My grandson won't drink his milk and I'm
floundering through *energy* and *you need* and the

weight of insistence.  When he kicks his shoe against
the corner floorboard—a light tap, really—eyes slant,

when he says *That makes me uncomfortable*
face pinched with audacity and the meaning

of milk, I sense a language between us.
He likes to find places on maps, makes me guess

where he'll land, no hints allowed.  Success is a place
I would never think of.  We're all gone

to our corners, kicking at the odd
rules we've come up with, trying to find

something less heartless than drinking alone.
The real obstinance, a belief in maps as meaning

more than the world can add up to.
He left for school, glass full.

March 2009

## Just Arrived

Only days old, in my dream you're already nine months
and I'm upset.  How could I have missed

those precious months?  Of course I didn't lose them
they weren't ours, they were your long time of

slow design, watery ride, your sea inside, where we
couldn't reach you but you were always held

where you taught us patience, faith, where
we saw your femur, bladder, your busy heart

in grainy sonogram blur, nothing like
this bloody thigh the midwife wipes

fleshy life.  Those months were why you're here
hot and silky, the whole of you

your dark eyes astounded by light.
May we always be so amazed.

October 28, 2008

# Falling

It's a wobbly world.  To clutch the couch,
stand tippy-toe, whack the blue and red

plastic train, to plie and bounce
is to chance a hard end.  A buckled knee,

an arm thrown too wide, and all is
lost: a crumpled flailing, soft head

smacks wood, a shriek, a swooping mom,
screams and kisses, consolation

against the tough job of being
upright.  The experienced among us

fail to find delight and grief on
such ordinary ground.  We walk

unremarkably into another room,
into the diluted days we call July,

August, another year, while here
on these floorboards a future

of risk and gain hovers in some
persistent balance.  She grabs an edge

of blue couch, thrusting herself up
with that balletic knee-bending,

that triumphant face, palms slapping
the cushion without a thought

to what's ahead.  To continue is what
matters, the daily graceful stumbling.

July 2009

# Crying Spot

Good idea.  Keep sorrow contained.
Circumscribe the broadcast of pain.
Above the din of story-time, of autumn leaves
sopped in glue, a scream of indignation.
At the teacher's finger-point
she runs over, stands in her circle,
belts out the fury of a grabbed book
the misery of sharing.
*OK, I'm done.*
Grief is quick
with so little yet to cry for.

November 2010

# 4.

New Poems—2003-2010

# Cleaning in Spanish

Because I ask
too many questions

and behind the refrigerator
would you mind.

How did I end up on this side
of payment

between the sink and the stove
her dark eyes close against the misunderstanding

she understands too well.
Sponges scour a takeover of mold

armies of bottles, astringent
air, our hazarded, ineffectual repair

lost as soon as we speak
the language that can't be gleaned

from first greetings
lugging in her load, buckets and rags

equipment that will settle
how it is.

A transfer of grime, my floors cleaner
her rags darker

she carries them away.

# Identity Theory

"The identity theory asserts that there is
not a relationship between two distinct
entities, only one entity for which we
seem to have two modes of expression."
—Daniel N. Robinson, philosophy professor

I stashed a bag of moldy boots under
the stairs, worn forty years back

my feet smaller, not yet
tired.  They seemed necessary

to salvage, powdered in mildew
or at least to let rot

while still beneath my feet, joining
the collection down there

young faces floating Ophelia-like, drowning
under boot-stomped planks.

How do we move from one body to
another, from all that damp

walking to this need for preservation
saving the spores that will

cover us over.  Philosophy
doesn't comfort, it shreds

like the rest of us, like
wet paper holding together ideas.

I'm up here, sorting
wringing, straddling these

rivers, trying to stay above
disintegration.

They kept me dry, those boots
that face gone as water.

# Marin Hillside, 1975

A snapped photo becomes iconic rather than random.
Atop the hill I had a 360 view
husband and small child distant.
My arm wave cuts the light, signaling
descent or height or the divide.

When the sun went down it took me
with it.  Years vanished before I saw
that rise again, shorn of any silhouette
I could imagine.

Work and love, Freud said, our lifelong dilemmas,
but I think it's all the expanses, those ravishing
spaces that catch us

sun-framed and radiant, possibility
in every direction.  Long jean-clad legs, long arm
waving, jubilant, before that stunned look back

at the gap between us.  I flew down, swung
my child to my chest, grabbed my husband's hand
giving love its careening moment.
To be happy, wear blinders.
I did, for awhile.

# Brando's Island

First the question why would he want it
not so obvious as it seems, perhaps
about distance or dreams.

He wanders to the edge, the wind-lashed beach
reconfigures, the discarded

arrives, plastic fishing line, bottle caps
persistent as trade winds hurled
over oceans to scour his shore
washing up

waste and appetite, the dream of
sandy languid nights.  Does he think
of that stage left behind

or only of being tired and not
having gotten it right, the longed-for land
marred by nearness.

You see all sides from here.
Rain pounds.  Sand trails everywhere.
He'll end up sodden and gone
owning the world from horizon to

horizon with no more room
to stride than a
cat in a well, wet and yowling
at a distant bright sky.

# How Close

"Those who came closest did not
come close."
—John Ashbery

You who came as close as skin allows
are not the one, our ineffective

lips, fingers, tongue,
nor that lost one from early days who

for all our sparked rambunctious love
was the furthest from what lay within,

nor the one who grew with my own blood
touching inner places even

lovers cannot reach.  Not love
or attachment but the loss of these

gives entry, leaving us more than
we are alone, doubling back

to ourselves, inspired and blind
as fish throngs in balletic slip-shape,

sublimely spliced in their dash
from prey, a frenzied joining

fueled by hunger and terror.

# Boundary Conditions

"The universe has no boundaries."
—Stephen Hawking

Thin as a veined eyelid, as hot
translucent skin
these crucial lines we've drawn
resisted and insisted on

These separate selves dangerously brushed
in love and dangerously separate
again, we're told don't exist.
Your atoms, mine, one galactic
wholeness, a god-mind of unified
creation, boundaries

a fallacy of those blinded
by love of what is seen or touched—
conditions: rough.

Of course human forces differ
from the cosmic, no speed of light
we're slow and so
content with what we
blindly know.

## Late

Love gone angry again.  Perhaps Kalua
and cream, smooth

and the right mix.  Let's sit
let's have an amnesiac, slow

draw, no talk.
It's an effort to silence alarm

but necessary.  Out the window
wires slice a salmon sky.  We cut up

what we prize, held in the beginning
with hope, miles of open

view ahead, free of grievance.
The error is in accumulation.

So much wisdom collected
by the unwise.

We keep walking, ten years
twenty, past the place

we leave behind and the one
we've yet to find.

# Cloud Computing

When I heard what he
did for a living I wondered
if there was weather
there and if so

for whom, and would it spare
the rest of us down here
its restless energies contained
like ions potentiating

rain, lusty and swarming
and where is this rainless cloud
so full of its own potential
it's become indispensable
he says, since his job depends—

We've become remote and
we like it that way, our
billions of megabytes pulsate
elsewhere, we sleep soundly

no need for wet stones
cold to the touch when I find
the dropped coin flashing
in a gravelly gutter puddle.

# Things I'd Never Tell My Mother

After my mother died we began talking almost every day. She wasn't about to leave behind an empty and unperturbed silence. Her presence would be noisy and absolute. First the dream in which she snores loudly in the next room, behind a thin, transparent wall, keeping me awake. Then the one in which she stamps her foot in anger, complaining, "You're not listening to me!" Then the parade of visits, of houses and beds and alcoves and rooms she fills with her nighttime presence, until I understand she is going to be my companion, as lasting as a brick hearth.

I wasn't sorry to have her around. We had only begun talking, it seemed. I'd forgotten why we didn't talk more. The reasons seem remote and forgettable, having more to do with a certain geography than anything else. I didn't get over her way. But now it's easier. She's always close by and there's no limit of time. The funny thing is I think we enjoy these conversations more than any of the past. We say what we think. Sometimes she's upset, sometimes sobbing. There's lots of blame, and just as often a smile that floods sunlight everywhere. Sometimes I hand her a knife and the kitchen is in disarray, stacked with grimy cups, and I think I can never forgive her this mess, this linoleum where my shoes stick to the floor. Then she's laughing and handing me a shell in a tiny envelope and I know it's a keepsake I can pull out anytime I need it. There are the angers you think will never settle, and the longing that will never leave, the empty windows and distant freeways, and when she's suddenly off to the shore, leaving me with those dishes, I know I'll have to tell her, and that now I can.

# Desire

My neighbor's cascading drape of Chinese elm
its tangled bent-over tresses, that glinty emerald

dense as thatch, ungainly perhaps, but a resting
place for mind and eye.  When I spied the belted

chainsaw, the slings and pulleys monkeying
through branches, I begged, *Not my*—

No mercy.  The landlady wants safety
the tenants light, the arborist his art

my desire a slight affair.  Limbs tumbled
shreddings of plump greenery, a woodsy

dust as from a shaken nest, clearing
from encumbrance a stately denuded trunk

upthrust branches carving the sky
spare arcs and curves, bright doorways.

Balconies appeared, windows, a water heater
on a screened porch, an orange box of Tide.

That night I sat in a perplexing light, porch light
moonlight, a high crown of leaves swaying

above, trying to figure where beauty lies and
how to desire what is.

# They Put a Signal at the End of Our Street

Now our evenings flash red and
green, like extremes of thought
that bother us with their

clarity.  We've lost
our shifting sky
until those bushy spruce grow

higher, which they will as we
slow and fade, daily
reminded of the start and

stop to things.  This garish
Christmasy display, this steady
alarm meant to save us with

civility.  We close the drapes
against anything so sure.
Let the streets offer

up their order, let the day
settle to bleating horns and
impatience contained

let the world convince itself
it can be restrained.
I'd rather drift in the

uncertainty of dusk's turn
gold to grey, some nights
rain or fog.

## Across a Night Sky, Ghosts

When strange recollections
    tear the weave

letting through
    slipstream

an addled concussion of stars
    showering their load

of loss and remembering,
    tailings, silvery

and sharp, it can rain
    too heavily.

Houses are needed
    battened and caulked

against the
    ripped sky.

There's enormity
    and there's life

and this small
    place we build

will suffice.

## Since Then

Since then we've slowed
and worse,
a slim contentment

ready to turn at a whim.
We are no longer sure
or surprised

often advised, our pastime
watching the imagined
shorten, our grace

forgetting and
remembering.  Some days
bring apples

other sweetness.
A grandchild appears,
two.  We continue

even these bursts of
momentary shine falling
each one, behind.

# Explosions: New Year's Eve Day, 2010

### 1

We are parts, scattered
We are not whole
Mending happens in another world
forgotten or wistfully recalled
summer nights stunned by the beauty of fireflies

I'm ill, in bed, and the world
is a chaos of chance implosions
If I'm lucky, dinner of ham and crumbly
cheese under a low sky
An arm falls, plates lower themselves to the table
one leg follows another as if logic prevails
We are pieces, crumbs

### 2

Quiet is local and prized
Today everyone naps
before waking to dance whatever they dance these days
to find tongues of love, a salve
as red-green fireworks shatter the sky
beautiful and atomized
We party, then leave
what we manufacture in moments
of need

### 3

Here a small drama suffices for misery
an illness, an argument
Who's to measure suffering, I wouldn't dare

The he-went-to-the-store-for-cigarettes-didn't-come-back
or the affair, broken leg, ski-lift accident type
Who's to say
each one slammed
It's quiet today, but misleading

Elsewhere rotor blades salvage
or savage a night
Nigeria, Liberia, Iraq, Spain
the names rain down
in evening display
with commentary, photos, sound
Technicians put them together
so we can understand in pieces

4

There are no illness conversations
only monologues, terse, succinct
More soup please, and socks
not philosophical
The ill get to the point

If time were the folds of a ballerina skirt
or the peeled back layers of something, I don't know what
I have something to say about time
It feels permanent and stuck
In illness the body implodes cell by cell, and daily
Days are to get through, cold is cold
no tuning out

No Sadness in This Poem:
Balboa, 1962

We knew little so we were happy, Dee Dee and I
buddies grabbing an amber sunset, a cousin's speedboat

flying past silent buoys, last warning before open ocean
above the weight of all that water, something I wouldn't
have thought of then.

"What I would like to experience most of all
would be to find myself freed, even if only
for a moment, from the weight
of my body," wrote Holocaust survivor Primo Levi

before dropping to his death in his apartment stairwell.
We flew, banging each watery crest in a blaze
of frothy sparks, each smack on fiberglass a thrilling
jolt, toe to head, cement-hard water

a buoyant road into light.
Later, dancing in someone's crummy backyard
concrete and shaggy bushes that seemed the only

place to be, in cut-offs and we didn't care
hot night air, we threw our bodies forward
drunk on watusi and our own best life

and then we left and that boat was somebody else's
drifting toward its water-logged end
strange and bereft.

## About the Author

Dorothy Wall (www.dorothywall.com) is author of *Encounters with the Invisible: Unseen Illness, Controversy, and Chronic Fatigue Syndrome* and coauthor of *Finding Your Writer's Voice: A Guide to Creative Fiction*. She has taught poetry and fiction writing at San Francisco State University, U.C. Berkeley Extension and Napa Valley College, and for 25 years has run a writing consulting business in Berkeley. Her poetry, essays and articles have appeared in numerous journals and magazines, including *California Magazine, The Writer, Witness, Bellevue Literary Review, Sonora Review, Under the Sun, Puerto del Sol,* and *Nimrod.*

Printed in the United States of America

www.ingramcontent.com/pod-product-compliance
Lightning Source LLC
Chambersburg PA
CBHW032026090426
42741CB00006B/741